# GOD
# MOMENTS
# IN TIME
™

## By Thomas E. Brewer

ISBN 978-0-9723261-4-8

LCCN 2005904464

ATTENTION CORPORATIONS, UNIVERSITIES, COLLEGES, AND PROFES-SIONAL ORGANIZATIONS: Quantity discounts are available on bulk purchases of this book for educational, gift purposes, or as premiums for increasing magazine sub-scriptions or renewals. For information, please contact

ProActive Faith Publishing™
PO Box 2394
Oklahoma City, OK 73101
(405) 602-0817

Website: www.ProActiveFaith.org
Email: publishing@proactivefaith.org
ProActive Faith Publishing™ is a division of ProActive Faith Ministries™, Inc.
ProActive Faith Ministries™ & ProActive Faith Publishing ™ and their logo and God Moments In Time™ are trademarks of ProActive Faith Ministries™, Inc.

This book is dedicated to my Dad and Mom.
Thank you for all your support and
encouragement over the past 31 years.
If it were not for your support I would have
never been able to start my ministry.
Love you very much!
Thomas

# *Acknowledgements*

Thank you Jesus, my Lord and Savior, for all you have done for me! Most of all I am thankful for your gift of salvation and for calling me to the ministry! You give me the ability to continue each day. I pray that I will be faithful to your calling on my life!

Mark R. & Don C.: Who would have ever thought that a cup of coffee would have been a "God Moment" in our lives? It was how we met and the ministry that has followed that gave me the idea for this book. Thank you for all you have meant to me these past few years. You guys are truly my brothers!

Kerry R.: Thank you for your support, your encouragement, and the knowledge you bring to the Board. You always are there to help answer any questions I might have. Mary, thank you for letting Kerry be a part of this ministry!

James L.: Who would have ever dreamed that in 1995 I would be writing a book? Thank you for all you have done for me over the years. You have always encouraged me to be just what God has called me to be. For the countless hours I have spent with you, Cindy, Hannah, and Jordan, I have been truly blessed.

Chris J.: Thank you for everything you have done over the years. Since OBU you have listened to my dreams for being in this type of ministry. Thank you Angela for allowing Chris to dream with me! Brother I look forward to seeing what God continues to do in your life and family in the years to come.

Rodney P: I thank God for bringing you and your family into my life! You always push me to be all I can be for God. Thanks for not letting me quit this book when the writing was hard. You and your family are truly a blessing in my life.

Maxine: For your support and encouragement I am truly grateful! You were the first to read part of the manuscript and gave me the encouragement to continue. I thank God for your daily support.

Dr. Smith: Thank you for your countless hours of hard work on this project! You have continually encouraged me to always be a learner. Thank you for the challenge! Your encouragement and support is priceless.

Brad P.: Thank you for your creative spirit! You have always been a support and encouragement to me and this ministry. Thank you for your hard work on this project.

Mr. Springfield: As a High School Senior you showed me the enjoyment of writing. You saw my God given ability and gave me the dream of writing. Thank You!

Mark L.: Thank you for all your help and support! You are a great example of a servant of God. I have watched you faithfully serve my ministry and others behind the scenes. Thank you for allowing God to use your life for His purpose!

The Supporters of ProActive Faith Ministries: Thank you for all you have done for our ministry. You have made this project and many others possible. I thank God each day for your support. You are truly a blessing!

# Contents

# Foreword
## by
## Jay McSwain

*I*f you are looking for a book to read that uses big words that need a dictionary or thesaurus to understand their meaning then God Moments In Time is not for you. However, if you are looking for a book to read that is simple, yet profound then this is a book for you.

There are few books that I read in basically one sitting. God Moments In Time is one of those books I could not put down. I was captivated by the nuggets that Thomas Brewer brought to the surface in the Scriptures, but even more captivated in how he moved from thousands of years ago to present day life situations that we as Christians can apply to our lives. For example, in chapter five, one nugget was drawn from Genesis 24:10-20. This is the story of Rebekah drawing water for the camels of Abraham's servant sent to find a wife for Issac. It was pointed out that there were most likely 10 camels and that a camel drinks up to twenty-five gallons of water each day. Rebekah physically drew up with a jug, approximately 250 gallons of water, for the servant's camels. The point in the story was to show the extraordinary kindness of Rebekah to a stranger. The chapter ends with a challenge that we can and should show kindness to strangers we meet every day. Throughout the entire book you will learn interesting and insightful facts about biblical culture and customs, but will be shown the practical application to your life through these insights.

As I was nearing the end of God Moments In Time I kept thinking that I would like to have just the questions that were asked in each chapter. At the end of the book there are five questions for each chapter. Some of the questions will take you back to the Bible and others will challenge and motivate you in your personal walk with the Lord. God Moments in Time coupled with the questions at the end of the book would make an excellent six week small group study.

The number one reason I recommend this book is because of the way Thomas handled the Scriptures. Too often today Christian speakers and authors take a small portion of the Scriptures and shape the text to meet a perceived need in the lives of individuals. This type of speaking and writing takes little if any time to help the believer understand the Scriptures, but uses the Scriptures to jump off into what could be found in any secular self help section of book-stores. This does not happen in God Moments In Time. It takes you back to the story of Abraham's servant in Genesis 24 and teaches you how God uses events in life that can become doors of opportunity that shape not only your lives, but the lives of countless individuals, many of whom you may never meet.

God Moments In Time will not only help you recognize God moments, but will teach you how you can live a life that allows you to experience God moments on an everyday basis. It is refreshing to read a book that uses Scripture as the beginning and the end in teaching us how to open doors of opportunity through everyday events in our lives.

***Jay McSwain***
President and Founder
PLACE Ministries

## CHAPTER ONE

# The Hinges in Life

*I* remember the little white house I lived in while a student in college. It was a two bedroom one car garage house. On the outside it appeared to be in great shape -- white siding, nice windows. Upon entry I soon realized that it needed some help -- a lot of help! It was truly a fixer-upper. I knew I had a task in front of me before I would be able to move in.

As it happened, my first semester I attended class in the morning and in the afternoons I worked on the house. In the days preparing to move in, I did some touch-up work. In the little hallway to the bedrooms there was a cabinet for blankets and towels. This cabinet had a couple of doors on it which needed to be painted. I began to put the paint on the doors and the door frame. In the process, I also painted over the hinges of the doors. At the time it did not seem like a big deal. A few days later I saw the results of painting over the hinges. *The doors would not open!* They were sealed shut. The paint had dried and in the process sealed the grooves of the hinges. The doors were unable to open because the hinges could not function properly.

I soon realized that I had a new task in front of me -- to get the doors open! It took time, but I was able with the help of a screw driver to get the paint out of the grooves of the hinges. The result of getting the paint out of the grooves was that the doors could then function properly. The hinges were scratched and still had paint on them in some places but the doors would open!

As I think back to that time in my life, I am reminded of what I heard as a young minister. *The great doors of opportunity swing on hinges called obedience.*[1] I must ask a question: "How many times have we painted over the hinges in life?" It is not actual paint we use, but rather the sin in our lives. If I have allowed sin to enter my life and have not confessed it and asked for forgiveness, the same is true of yours. Have you "painted over the hinges" with unconfessed sin? The doors of opportunity are unable to open in my life and yours.

As I look back over the ten plus years of ministry, I see that God has done some incredible things in my life. God has opened doors of opportunity in very unique ways. There have been events in my life that seemed normal at the time, as normal as any

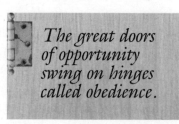

*The great doors of opportunity swing on hinges called obedience.*

other, but in fact they were full blown **God Moments in time.** I define a God Moment as *an event in life which God uses to open a door of opportunity that will change the direction of your life and possibly impact eternity.*

Just think about people who have been faithful to God and their impact on eternity. What if Billy Graham had not been faithful to the call of God on his life. There were times in the life of Billy Graham in which he could have gone a different direction than what God desired for his life. Billy Graham was faced with the choice of being in politics or continuing as an evangelist. He was being urged to run for the United States Senate by his supporters, but he had a choice to make like each of us have when faced with a cross road in life. *He refused to run for United States senator in his home state of North Carolina when supporters suggested it and then applied pressure, trying to make him conform to their wishes.*[2]

> *A God Moment is an event in life which God uses to open a door of opportunity that will change the direction of your life and possibly impact eternity.*

The faithfulness of Billy Graham and the Billy Graham Evangelistic Association has meant that countless numbers of people have come to faith in Christ. All would agree that the faithfulness of Billy Graham has impacted eternity.

Take a moment to think about the person who led you to Christ. Maybe it was a youth pastor or a Sunday school teacher. What if that person had not been faithful to the God Moments in his or her life? The question is "will we be willing to allow God to use those moments to affect our lives and possibly others?"

Think about your life. Has there been an event in which God has opened a door of opportunity, possibly a new job, new friendships, or anything else in the most unique circumstances and ways? I can personally say, "yes." There have been countless times where God has brought people across my path and it became one of those God Moments in time. Many times those moments have occurred during regular activities I do every day.

As a senior in high school, I was in a leadership position that required that I help at an annual youth conference. On the second morning of the conference I arrived early and there was a man unloading some boxes from his car. I asked him if he needed some help. He said "yes" and I helped him get the boxes into the arena.

Later that morning I had a chance to talk with him. I discovered that he was doing another conference in a couple of weeks and could use some help. I agreed to help him. Through that experience, God opened the door for my first ministry position. My start in ministry can be traced back to carrying a box for a man one December morning.

Another such event happened when I stopped by a coffee shop. Through that normal event in my life, God brought across my path two men who have changed my life and ministry. As a result of meeting these two men, God, in turn, opened a door of ministry that I could never have opened without them or at that moment in time. As we go through our lives events take place which, years later, we look back on and realize that it was one of those God Moments in time.

As you read the pages of this book, I invite you to enter into one of the most incredible journeys in the entire Bible. When you see how the journey evolves through the pages of this book you might be able to relate to it in many ways. You will see the incredible faithfulness of a father, of a young woman, and of a servant. Most of all, you will see the faithfulness of our God.

I pray that through this story of obedience and hope, you see the possibilities in your life. Remember, you too can experience many God Moments in time. As you read, let it encourage you to be open to God working in and through these unique moments in your life. As you look at the servant of Abraham, be challenged to be faithful to God in the small things. Remember, it might be one of those hinges opening a door in your life. All that is required is that we are faithful in those moments and allow God to change lives in radical ways.

*All that is required is that we are faithful in those moments and allow God to change lives in radical ways.*

*When is the last time you oiled your hinges?*

## CHAPTER TWO

# *The Faithfulness of the Father*

*T*o begin the journey we need to first look at the background of a father. Abraham, whose name was originally Abram, was given a promise from God-- that he would be the father of many nations. "I will make you into a great nation and I will bless you; I will make your name great, and you will be a blessing" (Genesis 12:2). "I will make your off-spring like the dust of the earth, so that if anyone could count the dust, then your offspring could be counted" (Genesis 13:16). When God spoke to the heart of Abram, the promise at that time looked impossible.

This was because Abram and his wife (Sarah, whose name was originally Sarai) had no children. Abram also had questions about the situation. "O Sovereign Lord, what can you give me since I remain childless..." (Genesis 15:2a). For Abram to become the father of many nations he would need a son. The Lord replied to the questions of Abram. "Look up at the heavens and count the stars -- if indeed you can count them. Then he (the Lord) said to him, 'So shall your offspring be'" (Genesis 15:5b).

As we look at Abram's life we see that he had a question for God. Let us remember that it is okay to ask God questions. There are times when the situation I am facing does not make sense. I go to God with a question about the situation, and this is okay. It is not disrespectful. Remember that God is not going to get mad when we ask Him questions to help us understand Him and His way better.

Again when Abram was ninety-nine years old, God confirmed his promise to him that he would be the father of many nations. "The Lord appeared to him and said, 'I am God Almighty; walk before me and be blameless. I will confirm my covenant between me and you and will greatly increase your numbers.' Abram fell facedown, and God said to him, 'As for me, this is my covenant with you: You will be the father of many nations. No longer will you be called Abram, your name will be Abraham, for I have made you a father of many nations. I will make you very fruitful; I will make nations of you, and kings will come from you. I will establish my covenant as an everlasting covenant after you for the generations to come, to be after you" (Genesis 17:1-8).

> *Remember that God is not going to get mad when we ask Him questions to help us understand Him and His way better.*

Not only did God change his name to Abraham but with the renewing of the covenant He changed the name of his wife to Sarah. "God also said to Abraham, 'As for Sarai your wife, you are no longer to call her Sarai; her name will be Sarah. I will bless her and will surely give you a son by her. I will bless her so that she will be the mother of many nations; kings of people will come from her'" (Genesis 17:15-16).

Abraham hearing that his wife would bear a son laughed at the words of the Lord. Abraham was one hundred years old at this time and his wife was ninety years old. Abraham fell facedown; he laughed and said to himself, "Will a son be born to

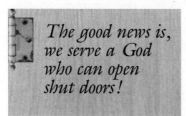

*The good news is, we serve a God who can open shut doors!*

a man a hundred years old? Will Sarah bear a child at the age of ninety?" (Genesis 17:17). They both were past the point of being able to bear children nor-

mally. For them to bear a son it would take God working a special miracle in their lives.

Like Abraham, many times in my life, God has given a promise when it seemed impossible from the world's viewpoint and from my own. At the time that God has spoken, the doors have been closed to that promise being fulfilled. Often the doors seem like they are sealed so shut that they cannot be opened. But the good news is, we serve a God who can open shut doors!

Have you ever thought about the purpose of a door? It is to open and close. Each morning as I am leaving my house for a day full of opportunities to serve the Lord I must open the door. Imagine what would happen if I attempted to leave the house without opening the door? My failure rate would be one hundred percent. Like the door that I painted shut as a college student, the door I exit through each morning has hinges. Only these hinges have never been painted! They work great, and without giving it a sec-ond thought, I open the door and walk out

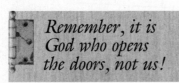

*Remember, it is God who opens the doors, not us!*

to my car. The key to the door working correctly is three important little items connected to the door and the frame. You guessed it -- the hinges!

A warning must be given as we look at doors in our lives that are shut. Many times these doors are shut because God does not want them to be opened in our lives, at least not at that moment in time. Remember, it is God who opens the doors, not us! As we will see later in this book, Abraham tried opening a door on his own. The result was a son, Ishmael, which was not the will of God for Abraham. We too, like him, will face the conse-quences of opening our own doors.

In life, as God gives promises and doors need to be opened, one thing can be certain: God is the one who controls the hinges. God opens doors where it seems like the hinges are painted shut. All God requires is the faithful-ness of his children.

*God opens doors where it seems like the hinges are painted shut.*

When it looks most impossible, like it did for Abraham and Sarah, that is when God comes through and opens closed doors.

Abraham and Sarah did have a son, whom they named Isaac. Even after God's promise was fulfilled he wanted to see if Abraham was faithful. When Isaac was still young, God spoke to the heart of Abraham and told him to take his son on a journey. It was on this journey that Abraham was to build an altar and sacrifice his son. I know what I might have done if God had told me that. "Remember God about the promise. I am to be the Father of many nations and that cannot happen unless I have a son." Abraham was faithful and God honored his faithfulness! As he laid his son on the altar and was going to sacrifice him, God provided something else, a ram, to sacrifice.

*God most of all desires a faithful servant; even in times when in human terms it does not make any sense.*

Isn't that how God works? He provides for his children in their time of need. God most of all desires a faithful servant; even in times when in human terms it does not make any sense. God provided the sacrifice for Abraham and Isaac in the same way he provides for you and me every day.

The promise that Abraham would be the father of many nations has been given but there is still a door closed. God was going to open a door in which an incredible journey would take place. Little did Abraham know, but he was about to send a servant on a journey that would turn into a "God moment in time."

*When is the last
time God let
you down?*

# The Journey Begins

The journey starts when Abraham, who is well advanced in age, goes to one of his servants. He had an incredible and important task for his servant to complete. His son Isaac needed a bride and his servant was going to play the key role in finding this bride. Remember the chapter that you just read, and the promise given to Abraham? In order for the promise of God to happen for Abraham, his son was going to need a bride. He would need to marry and have children.

This servant had a very unique status in relationship to all the other servants of Abraham. The Bible calls him "the chief servant in his household, the one in charge of all he had" (Genesis 24:2a). This was the "chief" servant who was the most important of all the servants of Abraham. The word "chief" is used in the New International Version of the Bible. In some of the other translations you might see the word "oldest" or "elder" instead of "chief."

What if there was someone in your house, a servant, who was in charge of all you had. What would his task and responsibility be? Would you trust this person? For me to place someone else in charge of all I have, I would need to have complete trust in that person.

This servant must have had this kind of trust in the sight of Abraham. One of the most important earthly possessions of Abraham was his son Isaac. He must have realized the magnitude of responsibility that would come with finding a bride for Isaac. This was one of the key elements related to the

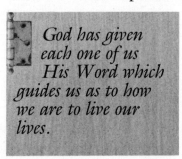

*God has given each one of us His Word which guides us as to how we are to live our lives.*

promise made to Abraham. It is only logical that the chief servant of the household would be trusted with this responsibility.

The high responsibility given to the servant demanded a vow. "Put your hand under my thigh. I want you to swear by the Lord, the God of heaven and the God of earth, that you will not get a wife for my son from the daughters of the Canaanites, among whom I am living, but will go to my country and my own relatives and get a wife for my son Isaac" (Genesis 24:2b-4). Did you see the requirement that Abraham placed on the servant in this vow? The servant could not find a bride in the country where they were living. The vow required that the servant would begin a journey to find Isaac a bride.

In our relationship with God, we desire that He will open doors of opportunity in our lives, but this requires that we obey. God has given each one of us His Word which guides us as to how we are to live our lives. The key to living a life like God desires from us is that we spend time alone with Him in His Word.

The question I asked when I first read this passage was, "Why did he put his hand under the thigh of Abraham?" This action represents the importance of the vow which the servant was taking. The action of placing the hand under the thigh of Abraham represents the giving of life. The request that Abraham was making of his servant required a deep commitment on his part. The requirement of this kind of oath from the servant shows the importance of the task before him.

I have found that many of the doors which God opens involves a process or a journey which takes place. Many of the journeys are over a short period of time, but then there are others which are much longer. It is in these longer journeys that I often grow deeper in my relationship with God. I wish many times that the same outcome could be achieved with the shorter journeys. I have a close brother in Christ who refers to these times as "refinement by fire moments." I confess that the long journeys are not my favorite, but they are the ones in which I grow most in my faith. I like the process to be short and sweet so that I might reap the rewards of the open door.

The servant had a question for Abraham concerning the instructions he was given. Like the servant, I find myself questioning God when He gives instructions. "The servant asked him, 'What if the woman is unwilling to come back with me to this land? Shall I take your son back to the country you came from?'" (Genesis 24:5). The servant had an honest question. He wanted to be sure that he was clear on the instructions of his master Abraham. Abraham made his requirements clear in his response: "'Make sure that you do not take my son back there', Abraham said, 'The Lord, the God of heaven, who brought me out of my father's household and my native land and who spoke to me and

> *We might not hear what we desired but we will know the desire of our heavenly Father.*

promised me on oath, saying, "To your offspring I will give this land"-- he will send his angel before you so that you can get a wife for my son from there. If the woman is unwilling to come back with you, then you will be released from this oath of mine. Only do not take my son back there'" (Genesis 24:6-8).

Did you notice that Abraham did not get upset with his servant for asking the question? The same is true of our God! He will not get upset when we ask Him questions. We might not hear what we desired but we will know the desire of our heavenly Father. Imagine the response of Abraham if the servant had not asked the question and took his only son back to the land of his father. It is better to ask questions so that you might truly know the desire of the master.

In the response which Abraham gave, there was a "release" for the servant of the vow he had made. Did you notice if the woman would not return with the servant he was then released from the vow? In the same way it is good to know that in our relationship with God we are not responsible for the results of the open doors. All God requires is our faithfulness.

Have you ever been in a situation where you gave the instructions but the results were not what you had desired? This happened to a youth minister friend of mine a few years ago. He was returning home from a wonderful week of youth camp with his students. As they pulled into a gas station he instructed one of the young men in his group to fill up their church bus with gasoline. They pulled up to the pump and the student had a choice of gasoline types to put into the bus. There were three types of unleaded and diesel. The student was given instructions to fill up the bus. He had assumed which type of gasoline the bus required.

*He would much rather we ask Him a question about a situation than just to proceed on our own assumptions.*

About ten miles up the interstate everyone on the bus realized the gasoline choice was not correct. The young man had assumed the big bus required diesel but the fact was the bus required unleaded. The result of his choice in gasoline was a bus that would not run properly. My friend would rather the young man had asked a question about what type of gasoline to use rather than just assuming. The same is true in our relationship with God. He would much rather we ask Him a question about a situation than just to proceed on our own assumptions.

When God opens a door of opportunity in our lives we are in essence taking a vow. We take the vow when we choose to enter through the open door. God desires such a commitment in our lives as did Abraham with his ser- 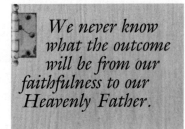 vant. You might be asking why? You never know but that door opening might forever change the direction of your life or it might impact eternity for countless numbers of people. We never know what the outcome will be from our faithfulness to our Heavenly Father.

> *We never know what the outcome will be from our faithfulness to our Heavenly Father.*

*Remember prosperity is success for your journey.*

## CHAPTER FOUR

# The Preparation of the Servant

The servant has made the vow to his master to go find a bride for Isaac but there is a preparation that is required to make this long journey.

"Then the servant took ten of his master's camels and left, taking with him all kinds of good things from his master" (Genesis 24:10a). This one verse sums up all the preparation of the servant for the task in front of him. You might be wondering, since there is not much detail in this verse, why it is so important.

Think about how you prepare for a trip. What all is involved in preparing to travel? You get a bag or suit case out of the closet and start filling it. You have to decide what you will need for the journey. You choose your clothes and all you might need when you are away. How much time do you spend getting ready for your trip? Is it ten minutes; is it hours; or perhaps a couple of days? It depends on the type of trip, the time that you will be away, and the task you seek to accomplish on your trip.

Have you ever been asked when you arrive at your destination how much time and effort you put in preparing for your trip? In all of my travels, I never recall being asked what I had done to prepare for the trip, or how much time it took. It is just assumed that if I have made a trip, no matter the distance, that I spent time preparing for the journey and the task I hoped to accomplish.

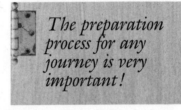

*The preparation process for any journey is very important!*

The real question is how important is your preparation? If you forget something, you might have to purchase it in order to accomplish what you traveled to do. The preparation process for any journey is very important!

The same was true for the servant. He prepared so he might be able to make the journey. Can you imagine what the servant went through as he prepared for this journey? No one really knows how much time it took to prepare for this journey but more than likely it was more than just a couple of hours. In fact likely it probably took days or even weeks to prepare for such a great journey.

How are you preparing spiritually for the doors of opportunity that God desires to open for you? Some will respond to that question like this: "I go to church every week, both Sundays and Wednesdays." Going to church is important in our Christian journey but how much time are you spending alone with God? Are you spending time in the Word of God and in prayer? For God to use us effectively we must spend time alone with Him. If you are not doing this, you are not learning His nature and will for your life. Time alone is key in your relationship with Christ.[1]

The servant had prepared for his journey and it was time to begin. "He set out for Aram Naharaim and made his way to the town or Nahor" (Genesis 24:10b). Do you find it interesting that the servant's journey is summed up in this one verse? In the world that we live in we might assume that this meant the journey just took one day. The fact is that the servant faced a very long journey. It is estimated that the distance the servant traveled to get to Nahor was 450 miles.[2]

On our modern interstate system we can drive 450 miles in about seven hours, but can you imagine walking this distance? The servant was faced with a journey that must have lasted days. I wonder if the servant ever had thoughts about turning back. I would have considered turning back and making some excuse to Abraham about why I could not complete the journey. But this servant had made a vow, and he must complete the journey.

When God opens a door of opportunity in your life and it requires a journey, do you ever think about turning back or quitting? I have, and there have even been times when I have abandoned the journey. When you remember the journeys that you have abandoned remember too that if you have asked God to forgive you, he has! We must not keep "beating ourselves up" for past mistakes that impact

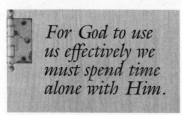

*For God to use us effectively we must spend time alone with Him.*

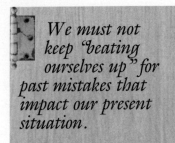

*We must not keep "beating ourselves up" for past mistakes that impact our present situation.*

our present situation. Move forward in the forgiveness of the Lord.

After the long journey, the servant was ready to complete the task that Abraham gave him to do. "He had the camels kneel down near the well outside the town; it was toward evening, the time the women go out to draw water. Then he prayed, 'Oh Lord, God of my master Abraham, give me success today, and show kindness to my master Abraham. See, I am standing beside this spring, and the daughters of the townspeople are coming out to draw water. May it be that when I say to a girl, "Please let down your jar that I may have a drink," and she says, "Drink, and I'll water your camels too" – let her be the one you have chosen for your servant Isaac. By this I will know that you have shown kindness to my master'" (Genesis 24:10b-14). The servant called on God to make his journey successful.

Just like the servant, we need to ask God to make our journey successful. As the doors of opportunity open we should desire success! My prayer each morning is *"God grant your servant success today!"*

*As the doors of opportunity open we should desire success!*

God desires that we have success in what He has called us to do. As the servant was praying that God would grant success to his journey, God was providing the provision. "Before he had finished praying, Rebekah came out with her jar on her shoulder" (Genesis 24:15a).

> *He has been preparing the answer before we even come to Him with the question.*

That is just like God! He has been preparing the answer before we even come to Him with the question. God has come through for me time and time again long before I ever expected. Remember that whether God answers our request before we have finished praying or if we must wait, He is still in control and He has our best interests in mind for our lives.

The servant is observing Rebekah and now he must see if this is God's chosen one for his master's son, Isaac.

*God will honor your preparation.*

## CHAPTER FIVE

# *The Kindness of Rebekah*

$I$t is amazing to see how God was preparing all the details of this incredible journey. God was working long before the servant prayed for success. God was already preparing Rebekah for her journey ahead.

Before we can look at the kindness of Rebekah we must know who she was and what qualities she had as a young woman. "She was the daughter of Bethuel son of Milcah, who was the wife of Abraham's brother Nahor" (Genesis 24:16b). This is a very important fact in regard to the vow the servant made to his master Abraham. In Genesis 24:4, Abraham says that this servant "will go to my country and my own relatives and get a wife for my son Isaac." In order for the servant to obey the command of his master and to be true to his vow he must get a bride for Isaac from among the relatives of Abraham.

The Bible also leads us to believe that Rebekah was an "eye catcher." "The girl was very beautiful, a virgin" (Genesis 24:16a).

I can hear the response of all who are single and who are reading this passage: "It must be nice."

Many single people are praying that God will open doors of opportunity in relationships. Let this journey remind to you that God is in control of your situation. He has a plan both for you and for your life partner. It might just be that as you are faithful to God and as He opens doors of opportunity, that He may lead you to your mate in life. Scripture's mention that Rebekah was very beautiful and a virgin reminds us again that God is concerned about every detail in our lives.

> *It might just be that as you are faithful to God and as He opens doors of opportunity, that He may lead you to your mate in life.*

If God is faithful in every detail in our lives we too must be faithful in every area in our lives, even in the details. God was able to call Rebekah to her journey because she was faithful in the normal everyday details of her life. "She went down to the spring, filled her jar and came up again" (Genesis 24:16b). During biblical times water was gathered from wells. In most towns there would be a well where all the people would come and draw water for their families. Verse 13 says the servant went to the spring where the daughters of the townspeople

> *I want to remind you again that God will often open doors of opportunity through the normal daily activities in your life.*

would come and draw water.

I want to remind you again that God will often open doors of opportunity through the normal daily activities in your life. It can happen in the "big" events of life, but most open doors happen in the midst of normal daily activities.

The servant hurried to meet her and said, "Please give me a little water from your jar" (Genesis 24:17). Little did Rebekah know, but she was about to encounter one of those "God moments in time." "Drink, my lord, she said, and quickly lowered the jar to her hands and gave him a drink" (Genesis 24:18).

Did you notice that Rebekah had to lower her jar in order to give the servant a drink? Think about this in the context of what she was doing. Going to the well was a daily routine for Rebekah. The uniqueness of this time was her encounter with the servant. Rebekah most likely assumed that her task of drawing water from the well was complete but in fact this was only the beginning.

> *Many times, when we believe we are at a point of completion, God is saying it is only the beginning of an incredible journey.*

Many times when we are on a journey in life we believe we are near the completion but in fact it is just the beginning. For Rebekah, drawing water from the well that day was the beginning of an incredible journey in her life. Many times, when we believe we are at a point of completion, God is saying it is only the beginning of an incredible journey.

Can you imagine what the servant must have been thinking as she gave her reply to him? His mind must have been running a million miles per hour. He must have been thinking that the request he made to God was coming true. You can almost imagine him wondering whether or not she was going to offer to water his camels. The anticipation must have been killing him.

"After she had given him a drink, she said, 'I'll draw water for your camels too, until they have finished drinking.' So she quickly emptied her jar into the trough, ran back to the well to draw more water, and drew enough for all his camels" (Genesis 24:19-20). It is worth noting that Rebekah was willing to go the extra mile in her kindness to the servant. She was willing to give the camels all they wanted to drink.

Have you ever seen a camel at the zoo? Have you watched him take a drink? I have seen some up close, and I would sure not like to draw water from a well for one camel, let alone ten of them. This was not a quick task for Rebekah; it took time and it was work. When you watch a camel take a drink you will see the water level in the tank go down.

Camels can drink up to twenty-five gallons each; for ten camels that is two hundred fifty gallons of water.[i] That is a lot of water even if you are just filling up a bucket with a hose; but to draw that much water from a well one jug at a time! The New King James version states that Rebekah used a pitcher to draw the water so she must have made many trips in order to water all these camels.

In verse 16 in the New Kings James Version it states that Rebekah "went down to the well, filled her pitcher, and came up." Did you catch the two key words in that verse, down and up? That means that she had a task that was more than just drawing the water from a hole in the ground. More than likely Rebekah had to go down to the spring and then walk back up to the camels.

Consider whether she ever thought about giving up. I can imagine that she was wondering if these camels would ever get enough water. She had begun the task and she was going to finish. Rebekah had given him a drink and also gave water to the camels to the point that the camels finished drinking. This shows the incredible kindness of Rebekah.

*God uses the events life that are hard to complete or that we might not enjoy as a way to open doors of opportunity.*

God uses the events life, that are hard to complete or that we might not enjoy, as a way to open doors of opportunity. I wonder, during the process of drawing water for the camels, if Rebekah ever wanted to quit? Did she get tired of going back and forth to the well for more water? However, it was her kindness to the servant that showed him that this was the one who was to be the bride of Isaac. It was because of her kindness that her life was going to change radically.

It is easy to be kind to someone that we think can help us in life, but we must be reminded to be kind to all we come into contact with each day. My father told me once about a man who was very well off financially. If you were to see this person though, you would never expect him to have much money. He lived and dressed like a normal ordinary person. One day this man went into a car dealership and was looking at purchasing a vehicle. He was dressed in bib overalls, nothing fancy at all. The young salesman saw the appearance of the man and thought that there would be no way he could afford the car. When the man asked the price of the vehicle the sales man priced it very high. He thanked the young man and walked away because the price was too high. Another sales person asked the young man what he had done. The young sales man was surprised to hear who this man was and that he most likely had enough in his pocket to pay cash for the vehicle. The young man had made a terrible error in judgment.

My father told me this story as a young man to show me that I should not judge a person by their outward appearance. I can remember being with my father so often and going to town for lunch. Often people would come to the table to visit with dad. Later I always would ask who they were. Many times I learned that the person at our table was, by the world's standards, a very influential person. Their appearance many times was normal. On the other hand many people who appear to be important are in fact not as important as they appear.

The young salesman ran out and said that he had made a mistake in pricing the vehicle. He now took the man seriously and priced the vehicle where it was a good deal. The man bought it. In fact he reached into the front pocket of his bib overalls and paid cash on the spot!

When the camels had finished drinking, the servant took out a gold nose ring and two gold bracelets. Then he asked, "Whose daughter are you? Please tell me, is there room in your father's house for us to spend the night?" (Genesis 24:22-23).

The servant needed to know whose daughter this

> *The servant realized that the request he made to God to grant him success had truly been fulfilled.*

was and if there would be room for his party to stay the night. "She answered him, 'I am the daughter of Bethuel, the son that Milcah bore to Nahor.' And she added, 'We have plenty of straw and fodder, as well as room for you to spend the night'" (Genesis 24:24-25). The servant realized that the request he made to God to grant him success had truly been fulfilled.

Not only had Rebekah shown incredible kindness in offering water to the servant and his camels, but now she was going to show her kindness again. She invited this servant to come and stay at her home. She was going to provide for his camels too. Remember the kindness of Rebekah as you continue reading this journey. Also think about how you can show kindness to people you meet every day.

*God expresses His love through kindness.*

## CHAPTER SIX

# *The Successful Journey*

*T*he servant was facing the reality of the moment that God had made his journey successful. In that moment the servant knew he had to give the praise to God for answering his prayer. "Then the man bowed down and worshiped the Lord, saying, 'Praise be to the Lord, the God of my master Abraham, who has not abandoned his kindness and faithfulness to my master. As for me, the Lord has led me on the journey to the house of my master's relatives'" (Genesis 24:26-27).

The servant knew that it was God and not his own abilities that made his journey successful. Knowing this the servant offered praise. What a great example he is to us today.

How many times have we gone to God and asked Him to meet a certain need in our lives. In the spring of 2002, my father was very ill and needed surgery to save his life. The doctors told us of the risk involved in him coming through the surgery. They told us to say our goodbyes because there was a very good chance that he would not live through the surgery. Leading up to the surgery, I prayed that God would bring him through this process. My days were consumed with prayer for the healing of my father. As the doctor took him into the operating room he told us that it would take around three hours. He was going to update us as he was in the process of the surgery around the one hour mark. An hour passed by, and no word came. About an

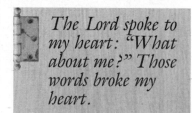

*The Lord spoke to my heart: "What about me?" Those words broke my heart.*

hour and a half into the surgery, I saw the doctor coming down the hallway toward us. I remember thinking that we were going to hear bad news.

The doctor explained that my father had come through the surgery but he would be in intensive care for several days. He continued to explain that the next several days would be "touch-and-go." He had come through, but he was going to have a long recovery ahead of him.

A few days later, while my father was in the Intensive Care Unit, the doctor came to check up on his condition. After he finished looking at my dad he met with the family. I remember saying to the doctor, "Thanks for saving my father's life!" Then, as I walked through the hallways of that hospital the Lord spoke to my heart: "What about me?" Those words broke my heart. I had given the doctor the praise that God alone was due. Just a few days, before, I had been crying out to God for a miracle. How easily we forget the blessings that God grants in our lives!

This servant had reached a point in his spiritual life that many of us need to reach in ours as well.

He did not wait to praise God later, but at the moment he realized that God had granted him the success he desired, he gave God the praise that He and only He was due.

Think about your life and the doors of opportunity that God has opened for you. Has there been something that you desired for so long that you thought you could not wait for that door to open? When it did open, did you give yourself the credit? Or did you, in that moment give God the praise? Look at the servant's example and remember that God is the one to whom praise is due.

> *Look at the servant's example and remember that God is the one to whom praise is due.*

Many times when something special has happened to me, as soon as possible, I wanted to tell someone what was happening. Often I found myself wanting to get in touch with my parents to tell them the great news. I assume the same was true for Rebekah. She realized that something truly special was taking place and she wanted to tell her family. "The girl ran and told her mother's household about these things. Now Rebekah had a brother named Laban, and he hurried out to the man at the spring. As soon as he had seen the nose ring, and the bracelets on his sister's arms, and had heard Rebekah tell what the man said to her, he went out to the man and found him standing by the camels near the spring" (Genesis 24:28-30). Did you notice anything interesting? It appears that Rebekah left the servant standing at the spring alone.

Imagine what must have been going through the mind of the servant. He had just seen God grant him the success that he so desperately desired and there he stood alone! Rebekah had offered him a place to stay for the night, and one can only assume that in her excitement she must have forgotten to take the servant with her.

I have seen a similar scene many times when around children who have just received a gift. Think about the last time you were at a child's birthday party or at Christmas time, when they are opening gifts. Countless times, a child receives a gift 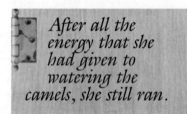 *After all the energy that she had given to watering the camels, she still ran.* that was really wanted. After removing the wrapping paper, and opening the box, they run off to play. They forgot one very important matter–thanking the one who gave them the gift.

I am sure each of us did that at some point in our childhood. We got so caught up in the moment that we forgot to say "thank you" to the person who gave us the gift we wanted so badly.

Did you notice the response of Rebekah when she realized the importance of the moment? She ran. Rebekah was so excited to tell her mother's household what happened that she ran all the way home. Think about the context of the events that have taken place. She had come to draw water as usual and then she provided enough water for the ser-

vant's ten camels. After all the energy that she had
given to watering the camels, she still ran. She had
to let her family know what was happening in her
life.

"'Come, you who are blessed by the LORD,' he
said. 'Why are you standing out here? I have prepared the house and a place for the camels.' So the
man went to the house, and the camels were
unloaded. Straw and fodder were brought for the
camels, and water for him and his men to wash
their feet. Then food was set before him, but he
said, 'I will not eat until I have told you what I have
to say.' 'Then tell us,' Laban said" (Genesis 24:31-
33). Laban had provided a place for the servant and
his camels to stay. It is interesting to see that the
servant was more concerned with telling Rebekah's
family why he was there, than he was with eating.

> *The servant
> was more
> concerned with
> the instructions of his
> master than he was
> with his own
> personal needs.*

The servant was more
concerned with the
instructions of his mas-
ter than he was with
his own personal needs.
This should remind
each of us to be con-
cerned first with the
desires and will of God
for our lives than with our own needs and wants.
The servant was determined to let Rebekah's family
know the desire of his master and the purpose of his
journey.

In Genesis 24:34-49, the servant recounts his
journey up to this point. I have often wondered
why the servant told the family of Rebekah the

whole story again. I believe the servant did it so that her family might see that God had blessed his journey. Remember just a few verses before these the servant gave the praise due to God. Here again he wanted God to get the glory.

This servant again can be an example to us as Christians today. What a witness for Christ it would be if we were this excited about telling the people we come into contact with about the goodness of our Heavenly Father. What would happen, if during a meal with someone we were this excited about telling them what God is doing in and through our lives? Can you imagine the surprise of the others at the table if we did not eat until we told them of the goodness of God? Let this servant remind us to put the spiritual things of life before the physical.

Rebekah's family soon realized that God had prepared and guided the servant on his journey. "Laban and Bethuel answered, 'This is from the LORD; we can say nothing to you one way or the other. Here is Rebekah; take her and go, and let her become the wife of your master's son, as the LORD has directed'" (Genesis 24:50-51).

Imagine what everyone must have been feeling during those moments as they heard what the servant had to say. There must have been a sense of excitement in the air. Laban and Bethuel knew that the Lord had brought this event together. "When Abraham's servant heard what they said, he bowed down to the ground before the LORD" (Genesis 24:52).

I am amazed at how the servant was again so quick to give the praise to God. Remember throughout the journey of life that when God opens doors of opportunity we should be quick to praise Him for His goodness!

"Then the servant brought out gold and silver jewelry and articles of clothing and gave them to Rebekah; he also gave costly gifts to her brother and to her mother. Then he and the men who were with him ate and drank and spent the night there" (Genesis 24:53-54a). There are two interesting facts to discover as you look at this passage. First you must remember in chapter four of this book, "The Preparation of the Servant," how the servant's preparation for the journey played a key role there. One of the reasons he worked so hard to prepare was because of the gifts that he was bringing for the young woman and her family. It was a custom in those days that the family of the husband would present gifts to the wife's family. These were not cheap gifts either, but very costly ones indeed.

*Remember throughout the journey of life that when God opens doors of opportunity we should be quick to praise Him for His goodness!*

The second point is that it is revealed in this passage that the servant was not alone on his journey. The phrase in this passage that speaks of the men, who were with him, shows that there was a group with him on this journey. Not only did Rebekah and her family show incredible kindness in allowing this man and his camels to stay the night with them

but also by showing hospitality to his companions.
They provided shelter and food to everyone. What
kindness this displayed!

*Success is what
God produces
through you.*

## CHAPTER SEVEN

# The Response of the Family

God had granted the servant success on his journey but a challenge was about to come his way. Rebekah's brothers and mother did not want her to leave immediately. "When they got up the next morning, he said, 'Send me on my way to my master.' But her brother and her mother replied, 'Let the girl remain with us ten days or so; then you may go'" (Genesis 24:54b-55).

There are two lessons to see as we look at these verses. First when God opens the door we should desire to go through it immediately. The servant desired to return to his master immediately.

God has opened doors of opportunity so often in my life, and each time my heart's desire was to go immediately. In August of 1999, a new ministry was opened for me. I remember where I was when I received the call to come see if I was interested in the ministry opportunity. I was driving a big moving truck to help one of my best friends pack up his summer camp program. I did not even know at that moment that God was getting ready to change my life and my ministry forever. I was offered an opportunity to serve as an associate director of a college ministry. I had been part of the program as a college student but never in my dreams ever thought of serving in that ministry. After a couple of hours of prayer I knew that God was leading me into this ministry. There was only one thing about taking this

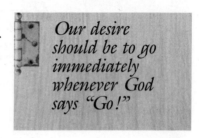

*Our desire should be to go immediately whenever God says "Go!"*

position. It was not to open for two weeks. I had to wait two weeks to start but my heart was ready to go immediately. Our desire should be to go immediately whenever God says "Go!"

Second, when God opens a door of opportunity many times the people we love most will stand in our way. The same was true for Rebekah. She had seen that this was an event ordained by God and she wanted to go. Sometimes the people who say not to go through a door of opportunity or just wait a few weeks are our family and very close friends.

There are many stories in the Bible where this takes place. Christ was even faced with this in His earthly ministry. When Jesus was telling the disciples that He was going to leave them they said, "No, it can't be." Jesus knew the heart of His Father and the will of the Father for His life. He was sent to earth for one reason. He was to die for the sins of the world.

Because of Christ's death on that cross, we can experience *"God Moments."* If Christ had never come to die for the sins of the world, we would have never known his salvation. It is because of our relationship with Christ that we are able to look back over the course of our lives and see the countless doors of opportunity that He has opened for us.

In the spring of 2002, God led me to start a nonprofit evangelistic ministry. This was a huge step of faith. I knew that God was leading me through this door of opportunity. I started sharing with my close friends what I felt God was calling me to do. Many of their responses were ones of concern. They did not mean to discourage me but they were concerned. How would I support myself? Could I wait a couple of years and save money? The questions were endless, but I knew in my heart what God was calling me to do. I took the questions of my friends seriously and then went to God in prayer about the matter. God will use people in our lives to help give us discernment in matters.

*Because of Christ's death on that cross, we can experience "God Moments."*

You might be asking how I knew that God was not using the questions of my friends to show me that this was not His will for my life. I spent many hours in

*If you believe God may be opening a door of opportunity in your life and you are questioning if it is His will, go to Him on the matter.*

prayer and reading the Bible. If you believe God may be opening a door of opportunity in your life and you are question-ing if it is His will, go to Him on the matter. We must remember that as children of God we are in battle against the spirits of darkness.

*Remember that above all else that we must go and follow the desires of God for our life even when our family and close friends question the timing!*

It might be that the questioning of our close friends is in fact being used by the spir-its of darkness to prevent us from going through the door of opportunity. Remember the definition of "God Moments in Time:" *it might change the direction of your life or possibly impact ETERNITY forever*. Seek God's opinion, and not the worlds. He will give His children clear direction.

The servant asked the mother and brothers to allow them to return. "But he said to them, 'Do not detain me, now that the LORD has granted success to my journey. Send me on my way so I may go to my master'" (Genesis 24:56).

They agreed to ask Rebekah what she desired. "Then they said, 'Let's call the girl and ask her about it.' So they called Rebekah and asked her, 'Will you go with this man?' 'I will go,' she said" (Genesis 24:57-58). Rebekah had a clear direction on the matter in her life and she was ready to go. Rebekah was willing to return with the servant even when her family questioned the timing.

Remember that above all else that we must go and follow the desires of God for our life even when our family and close friends question the timing!

*God's will should always win over intentions.*

## CHAPTER EIGHT

# *The Reward of the Journey*

As I look at the story of this servant I can relate it somewhat to my own life. There have been some incredible journeys and many times they have required a lot of work. Can you relate to the journey the servant had when you look at your life? The journey that one faces in life can range from completing a college degree to waiting for God to bring you your life's mate. One thing about a journey--at the end comes the reward!

I remember a reward that I got after a trip I took several years ago. One summer when I was in high school I served as a volunteer on a summer camp staff. I was able to serve a few weeks on staff, but I was also going to get to do something I had looked forward to for years. The camp had been taking backpacking trips and this year it was my turn to go. I could hardly wait for the trip to happen.

The time came for the trip and we were off to eastern Oklahoma for a four day backpacking trip. As we were being dropped off at the beginning of the trail it began raining. That was certainly an interesting way to begin a trip! Over the next three days I heard about the reward we would get when the van came to pick us up at the end. In the van there would be an ice chest full of water, milk, soda pop, and an assortment of candy. About the second day of the trip, being hot and tired, I began dreaming of this ice chest. Boy, I could hardly wait for the fourth day to come so I could have the refreshment of cold drinks.

When the fourth day arrived we woke up and had a great breakfast and packed our backpacks one last time. As we were walking out on the road, over the hill came the camp van. I could hardly wait to get in because of the ice chest that was going to be in the

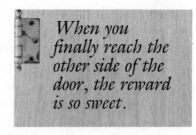

*When you finally reach the other side of the door, the reward is so sweet.*

back. I was not disappointed! The man who drove the van came through in a big way! He had packed one of the biggest ice chests I had ever seen! When we opened it we were so excited. On the top of the ice was an assortment of candy and under the layer of ice was every type of soda pop, water, and milk that the mind could imagine.

The reward of the long trip had finally come, and boy was I happy to see that ice chest! The same is true for the doors of opportunity that God opens. When you finally reach the other side of the door, the reward is so sweet. The same was true for the servant and the journey he had been on. Rebekah's family was sending her with the servant so she could become the bride for Isaac. "So they sent their sister Rebekah on her way, along with her nurse and Abraham's servant and his men. And they blessed Rebekah and said to her, 'Our sister, may you increase to thousands upon thousands; may your offspring possess the gates of their enemies.' Then Rebekah and her maids got ready and mounted their camels and went back with the man. So the servant took Rebekah and left" (Genesis 24:59-60). The reward would be when the servant returned to his master's son with Rebekah.

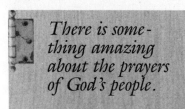

*There is something amazing about the prayers of God's people.*

Notice what Rebekah's family prayed for her in verse 60b? "Our sister, may you increase to thousands upon thousands." If you read the verses in Genesis 24 you will not see the servant telling Rebekah's family the promise from God that Abraham would be the father of many nations. In fact we have no account that the servant even knew of the promise God had made to his master Abraham. The servant was just doing what his earthly master had commanded him to do. He was being faithful!

When Rebekah was about to depart on her journey to become the bride of Isaac her family prayed a prayer of blessing over her. The point is that they prayed the promise God had made to Abraham many years prior.

There is something amazing about the prayers of God's people. I have many times prayed for a person by name and a certain situation in their life. Many times I did not understand why I was praying

for that situation. I just knew I was being led to
pray about a certain matter. Many times after praying for a period of time I would see the person I
was praying for and in our conversation I would
understand why I had been led to pray for that matter. When I was praying they were going through
that situation.

Could it be that, when Rebekah's family was praying for her to increase to thousands upon thousands, they really knew
what was taking place?
She would increase,
because God had
opened for her a door
of opportunity that she
was entering to
become a part of an
incredible promise

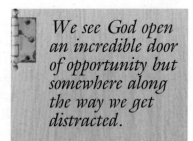

*We see God open
an incredible door
of opportunity but
somewhere along
the way we get
distracted.*

made to Abraham years before she and the servant
ever crossed paths.

Now that Rebekah was on her journey to meet
Isaac for the first time, I wonder if she ever had second thoughts. Her journey with the servant was not
just one day but several days. Like the journey the
servant had made to find her, she had to return on
the same four hundred and fifty mile trip. On this
long journey did she ever question what she was
doing?

When God has opened a door of opportunity for
me, and I am on the journey to the rewards, I have
often questioned whether I am really where God
wants me. It is amazing that we do this so often.
We see God open an incredible door of opportunity

but somewhere along the way we get distracted. It is through those times of distraction that we can lose focus on the journey that God has prepared for us.

During these times of journey in our lives we must seek God and His desires for us. We also need a group of people around us who are growing in their personal relationship with God. They will be an encouragement to us and an accountability team during times of discouragement and struggle.

The servant and Rebekah were about to see the reward of their faithful journey. "Now Isaac had come from Beer Lahai Roi, for he was living in the Negev. He went out to the field one evening to meditate, and as he looked up, he saw camels approaching. Rebekah also looked up and saw Isaac. She got down from her camel and asked the servant, 'Who is that man in the field coming to meet us?' 'He is my master,' the servant answered. So she took her veil and covered herself. Then the servant told Isaac all he had done. Isaac brought her into the tent of his mother Sarah, and he married Rebekah. So she became his wife, and he loved her; and Isaac was comforted after his mother's death" (Genesis 24:62-67). The long journey was over and the servant had returned with Rebekah, obeying the command of his master Abraham that he would not take Isaac to her, but bring her to Isaac.

Imagine this! While Isaac was out meditating he looked up and saw the camels coming.

Have you ever been out in the country where there are dirt roads? For much of my life, my family had a ranch in the country. It was amazing to see vehicles come down that dirt road. Long before we could ever see the vehicle we could see the dust being stirred up by the vehicle.

Most likely the same was true for Isaac. As he looked up he saw the dust rising from the earth as each camel and person took a step. Long before he could see Rebekah he saw them approaching. Can you imagine what Isaac must have felt in those moments? He knew about the journey the servant was on, and now approaching was his future bride.

*As we see God's reward for our journey coming closer, the excitement builds in our hearts.*

When Rebekah saw Isaac, she took her veil and covered her face. Both Isaac and Rebekah must have been nervous and excited in those moments before they were to meet for the first time.

As we see God's reward for our journey coming closer, the excitement builds in our hearts. When I saw that van loaded with cold refreshments approaching, the excitement was so intense that I could hardly stand it. After receiving the reward of the cold refreshing drinks, the long four day back packing trip was worth the effort.

The reward for the servant was seeing his master's son Isaac take Rebekah as his wife. It is truly amazing to see the rewards of the faithfulness of God's servants. The reward is God's promise fulfilled. Through Isaac and Rebekah, Abraham was going to become the father of many nations.

*The rewards of
your faithfulness
glorify God.*

## CHAPTER NINE

# Present Day Rewards of the Faithful Servant

*H*aving read through eight chapters of this book, you might be thinking that this is a very interesting story, and you would be right. But do you see the connection we Christians today have with this journey? Every day we are reaping the benefits of the faithfulness of this servant. Since the servant was faithful to his earthly master Abraham, we are reaping an incredible blessing each day.

What is this blessing you ask? Let me ask you a question that I asked countless individuals as I was writing this book: Who is Rebekah? Before you answer that question think "Big Picture."

Rebekah is the great-great (28 generations) grandmother of Jesus Christ! In the first chapter of Matthew we have the genealogy of Christ: "A record of the genealogy of Jesus Christ the son of David, the son of Abraham"(Matthew 1:1).*

This long passage ends with "Joseph, the husband of Mary, of whom was born Jesus, who is called

---

* *At the end of Chapter 9 there are the scripture passages and a diagram laying out the genealogy of Christ that is listed in Matthew 1:2-6.*

Christ" (Matthew1:16b). You see then that the faithfulness of the servant of Abraham still affects our lives today.

If you have trusted Christ as your Lord and Savior you have benefited from the faithfulness of the servant. It is because of the faithfulness of the servant that the line of descendants down to Christ could be born and Old Testament prophecy could be fulfilled.

> *However we might not ever in our lifetime see the full effect of our faithfulness in following God through those doors of opportunity.*

Think back again to the first chapter of this book and the definition of *"God Moments in Time." God Moments are events in life which God uses to open a door of opportunity that will change the direction of your life and possibly impact eternity.* We all would agree that the servant of Abraham was part of an event in time which has affected eternity forever!

One thing I desire is to see the effects of my journeys and works. What joy to see God working through my obedience especially through those *God Moments in Time.* However, we might not ever in our lifetime see the full effect of our faithfulness in following God through those doors of opportunity. They are no less real, and no less important for eternity.

Have you ever heard of a Sunday school teacher named Edward Kimball? In 1855, Kimball became burdened for a young shoe salesman. Kimball went to the shoe store on April 21, 1855, and shared

Christ with him.[1] That day, the young man, who
was named Dwight L. Moody, accepted Christ.
Years later, a student at Lake Forest College, J.
Wilbur Chapman, attended a meeting in Chicago,
and after the service received personal counseling
from Moody which helped him to receive certainty
of his (Chapman's) salvation. Later Chapman
became a friend and co-worker of Moody's. For a
brief time a former baseball player turned evangelist,
Billy Sunday, worked as assistant to Chapman.

*It was because of the faithfulness of a layperson who was a Sunday school teacher that a series of God Moments took place in several men's lives.*

Sunday helped orga-
nize Chapman's evan-
gelistic meetings. Billy
Sunday held an evan-
gelistic campaign in
Charlotte, N.C. in
1924 and a men's
prayer and fellowship
group grew out of
those meetings.
Originally known as
the Billy Sunday Layman's Evangelistic Club, it was
later renamed the Charlotte Businessmen's Club
(CBMC). This group was later instrumental in
inviting Mordecai Ham to Charlotte for his 1934
meetings. In those meetings, a young man gave his
life to Christ. That young man was named Billy
Graham.[2]

It was because of the faithfulness of a layperson
who was a Sunday school teacher that a series of
*God Moments* took place in several men's lives. Just
think what would have happened if Kimball had not
been faithful to his *God Moment*? Yet, because of his

faithfulness eternity has been impacted forever.

Do you think that Kimball ever thought of the far reaching effects of his faithfulness? It started with his faithfulness as Sunday school teacher which led him to share his faith. Many times God uses the "small" task in our lives to make the greatest impact, like he did with Kimball in 1855.

Does that mean that we should be disappointed if our task is small, or not do our best at what we are entrusted with? No! It means we are faithful even when we cannot see the big picture. You never know the impact that your faithfulness to a *God Moment* might have even many years later.

Do you think this servant ever dreamed of the eternal impact that he might have just by being faithful to his master Abraham? If he is like most people, probably not. He was probably just hoping

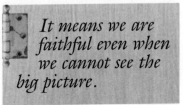

*It means we are faithful even when we cannot see the big picture.*

he would make his master happy. Just think what impact you could have, not only on your own life but countless other lives, if you are only faithful to go through your doors of opportunity.

We have seen an incredible journey unfold. It is amazing how this faithful servant has impacted eternity. Because he was faithful, God's promise to Abraham, that he would be the father of many nations, came true. Only eternity will reveal the full impact of this servant.

The same is true for us as we go through our journeys in life. We might not be able to see the

rewards of our faithfulness in the *God Moments in
Time*. Even when we cannot see the rewards of our
journey it is a comfort to know that because of the
character and faithfulness of God we can take heart.
We must remind ourselves that we are not going
through the doors of opportunity for the rewards
but because we are being faithful. We are to be
faithful and leave the fruits of our journey up to
God, the One who opens doors.

A question we must ask as we look at the faithful
servant is "what is his name?" As we consider how
he impacted human history the way he did, "we
wonder what is his name?"

The truth of the matter is we do not know. No
one can say for certain who this servant is. Some say
it is Eliezer who is mentioned in Genesis 15. "But
Abram said, 'O Sovereign Lord, what can you give
me since I remain childless and the one who will
inherit my estate is Eliezer of Damascus?' And
Abram said, 'You have given me no children; so a
servant in my household will be my heir.' Then the
word of the Lord came to him: 'This man will not
be your heir, but a son coming from your own
body will be your heir'" (Genesis 15:2-4). The truth
is it's just an assumption that the servant in chapter
24 is Eliezer. We cannot be one hundred percent
sure what his name is. About half of the commen-
taries say that it is Eliezer but others say his name is
not given. The time between chapter 15 and chapter
24 experts say was approximately 50 years. The fact
is, no one can be certain who the chief servant was.
That is the uniqueness of this story--that God
would use a man whose name we do not even know

to impact the lives of Isaac or Rebekah as well as the lives of people for generations to come. Such a man was used and found faithful, but today we can only can refer to him as the chief servant of Abraham.

*We must remind our selves that we are not going through the doors of opportunity for the rewards but because we are being faithful.*

# Matthew 1:1-16

A record of the genealogy of Jesus Christ the son of David, the son of Abraham: Abraham was the father of Isaac, Isaac the father of Jacob, Jacob the father of Judah and his brothers, Judah the father of Perez and Zerah, whose mother was Tamar, Perez the father of Hezron, Hezron the father of Ram, Ram the father of Amminadab, Amminadab the father of Nahshon, Nahshon the father of Salmon, Salmon the father of Boaz, whose mother was Rahab, Boaz the father of Obed, whose mother was Ruth, Obed the father of Jesse, and Jesse the father of King David. David was the father of Solomon, whose mother had been Uriah's wife, Solomon the father of Rehoboam, Rehoboam the father of Abijah, Abijah the father of Asa, Asa the father of Jehoshaphat, Jehoshaphat the father of Jehoram, Jehoram the father of Uzziah, Uzziah the father of Jotham, Jotham the father of Ahaz, Ahaz the father of Hezekiah, Hezekiah the father of Manasseh, Manasseh the father of Amon, Amon the father of Josiah, and Josiah the father of Jeconiah and his brothers at the time of the exile to Babylon. After the exile to Babylon: Jeconiah was the father of Shealtiel, Shealtiel the father of Zerubbabel, Zerubbabel the father of Abiud, Abiud the father of Eliakim, Eliakim the father of Azor, Azor the father of Zadok, Zadok the father of Akim, Akim the father of Eliud, Eliud the father of Eleazar, Eleazar the father of Matthan, Matthan the father of Jacob, and Jacob the father of Joseph, the husband of Mary, of whom was born Jesus, who is called Christ.

# Genealogy of Christ Diagram

## Abraham...

The father of Isaac --> Isaac the father of Jacob -->
Jacob the father of Judah --> Judah the father of Perez
--> Perez the father of Hezron --> Hezron the father of
Ram --> Ram the father of Amminadab --> Amminadab
the father of Nahshon --> Nashon father of Salmon -->
Salmon father of Boaz --> Boaz father of Obed --> Obed
father of Jesse --> Jesse father of King David --> David
father of Solomon --> Solomon father of Rehoboam -->
Rehoboam father of Abijah --> Abijah father of Asa -->
Asa father of Jehoshaphat --> Jehoshaphat father of
Jehoram --> Jehoram father of Uzziah --> Uzziah father
of Jotham --> Jotham father of Ahaz --> Ahaz father of
Hezekiah --> Hezekiah father of Manasseh --> Manasseh
father of Amon --> Amon father of Josiah --> Josiah
father of Jeconiah --> Jeconiah father of Shealtiel -->
Shealtiel father of Zerubbabel --> Zerubbabel father of
Abiud --> Abiud father of Eliakim --> Eliakim father of
Azor --> Azor father of Zadok --> Zadok father of Akim
--> Akim father of Eliud --> Eliud father of Eleazar -->
Eleazar father of Matthan --> Matthan father of Jacob
--> Jacob father of Joseph -->Joseph, the father of...

## Jesus Christ.

*Faithfulness produces eternal fruit.*

## CHAPTER TEN

# *Allowing God to Open Doors*

**Y**ou have read of an incredible journey and seen the faithfulness of the servant but most importantly the faithfulness of our God. Now you may want to see God open doors of opportunity in your life. In this chapter I want to discuss ways in which we can live our lives in such a way that will allow God to open doors.

Think back over your life. Whether you are young or old you have experienced the opportunity of gaining responsibilities. As a child growing up, your parents entrusted more and more responsibilities to you as they that saw you were ready for them.

I can remember one such event in my life. We did not live on a ranch, but our house had enough land that the city allowed us to keep a couple of cows there.

When I was beginning tenth grade, we had a baby calf that lost its mother. I was able to purchase the calf from my father. He told me of the responsibility that would come with taking care of a baby calf. I had to make a promise to my father to be responsible for it each day.

I was required every morning, even if it was raining or snowing, to wake up early enough before school to make a bottle of milk for the calf and feed it. The same routine would take place each night before I went to bed.

There is something interesting about a baby calf. A calf requires milk for several months when it is first born. This was not a task that took

> *We must prepare for the times in our life when God will open doors of opportunity.*

just a couple of weeks. As the calf grew, so did the responsibilities.

As my father watched me take care of this calf he realized that I could handle more and more responsibilities in my life. Before this time in my life, I wanted and desired responsibilities, but I was not ready for them.

In the same way we must prepare for the times in our life when God will open doors of opportunity. As you become an adult and move into your job or career, you must prepare. Many go to college to prepare for their life's work. In the same way we must prepare for God Moments.

It is amazing as an adult to see that the activity of preparation has not ended just because I have reached a level or age in my life. Preparation is a part of life. It is a task that continues as we grow. What we are going through today is in essence a preparation for an event to come later in life.

In the same way, for the servant to become the chief of all servants he had to be prepared. Abraham had to observe him and find him up to the responsibilities that would come with being the chief servant of all he had.

How do you prepare, you might be asking? First and foremost you must have a personal relationship with Jesus Christ. "Remain in me and I will remain in you. No branch can bear fruit by itself; it must remain in the vine. Neither can you bear fruit unless you remain in me" (John 15:4). This passage is about being connected to the true vine. A branch which is not connected to the main vine will never be connected to the true life source and bear fruit. In order for God to open doors of opportunity in your life you must be plugged into the source of life, Jesus Christ. If you never asked Jesus Christ to forgive you of your sins and to be your personal Lord and Savior I invite you to pray the following prayer:

*Jesus, I know that I am a sinner.*

*I ask you to forgive me of my sins.*

*I ask that you come and take control of my life and be my personal Lord and Savior.*

*From this moment on I will seek to serve you till the day you call me home.*

Whether you trusted Christ now for the first time or whether you have been a Christian for years, you are now part of an incredible journey! Remember that it is not the prayer that gives you the relationship with Christ but it is your repentance and faith expressed in the prayer. Remember, the evidence of a personal relationship with Christ is a changed life!

You also need to get connected to a Bible believing and teaching church that will help support and encourage you as you seek to follow Christ on your journeys in life. I have met too many people who tell me that they "practice church" on their own and are not  *I have never met a person who is not active in a local church who is experiencing God Moments in their daily life.* active members of a local church. When I begin to ask about their spiritual life it becomes apparent that they are not growing in their faith but are at a stalemate in life. As we continue to talk they admit that God truly has not opened doors of opportunity in their life since they stopped actively meeting with a group of fellow believers. I have never met a person who is not active in a local church who is experiencing God Moments in their daily life.

"I have hidden your word in my heart that I might not sin against you" (Psalm 119:11). You must also spend time alone with God. How will you know the heart of someone if you do not spend time alone with that person? The same is true of our relationship with God. We can never know his hearts desire if we are not spending time reading the Bible and time in prayer.

Also you must be faithful where you are. Many times we try to open doors of opportunity but it is not what God desires for our life. Every time I have stepped out on my own I have failed. As you will read in the next chapter, Abraham tried doing things his way and not God's way.

When I least expect it, God opens doors of opportunity in my life. This is the uniqueness of our God.

*Receiving God's grace will open doors in your life.*

## CHAPTER ELEVEN

# Don't Open Your Own Doors

As we discussed in the previous chapter, we must live a life that will allow God to open doors of opportunity for us. We must also guard against our human tendency to open doors on our own. All of us have done this at some point in our lives. We must be on guard of doing this. We must be content with God's plans, not ours!

Abraham tried doing things his own way. In the 16th chapter of Genesis, we see how Sarai (Sarah) told Abram (Abraham) to go and sleep with her maidservant Hagar. "The Lord has kept me from having children. Go, sleep with my maidservant; perhaps I can build a family though her" (Genesis 16:2b). Abram and Sarai were more concerned with the present situation in their lives than about the future that God had planned for them. Abram chose to follow the request of his wife instead of the heart and desire of God for his life.

Many times in our own lives people will attempt to direct our ways. Has anyone ever said you should do something, but you knew in your heart that was not what God desired for your life? I have experienced this many times. Also, many times I have chosen to go the way people were saying instead of going God's way. The problem was God desired for my life a different direction.

Have you ever chosen the world's ways? What was the outcome to choosing that way? Every time I have chosen the way of the world over the heart of God, I have always wished I could go back and choose God's way.

Abram must have rationalized in his mind the request of his wife. He could have thought, "It is okay because my wife said I can do it!" No matter how good your rationalization sounds, God's way is always better than our rationalization!

Many times we see the consequences of choosing the way of the world over God's way. Time after time I have regretted my choices but still time and time again I choose the way of the

> *No matter how good your rationalization sounds, God's way is always better than our rationalization!*

world. Every time, before going the way of the world, I have at some point rationalized why it is okay and go the way of the world.

"Everyone is saying to go through that door of opportunity." For me there is a mind game that takes place when I am hearing everyone saying to go. "Since everyone is putting their blessing on it, yeah it must be right." "These are great Christian friends. They read their Bibles, pray, and even go to church. That means it is right." Each of these thoughts are not reasons to go through door that seems to be opening. Only through prayer and seeking God can we determine whether or not we should go through what seems like a door of opportunity.

Hagar had a son for Abram which she named Ishmael. If you read Genesis chapter 16 you will see that when Hagar became pregnant Sarai became jealous. The decisions of Abram, Sarai, and Hagar, led to great pain in their lives. The choices we make in life not only affect our lives but the lives of the people we most love!

> *Only through prayer and seeking God can we determine whether or not we should go through what seems like a door of opportunity.*

Many times the pain of our choices comes sometime after we choose our own way. When Sarah bore Abraham his son Isaac, the jealousy continued to such a point that Abraham sent Hagar and her son Ishmael away. "Sarah said that the son, whom Hagar the Egyptian had borne to Abraham, was mocking, and she said to Abraham, 'Get rid of that slave woman and her son, for that slave woman's son will never share in the inheritance with my son Isaac'" (Genesis 21:9-10).

Can you only imagine what Abraham must have felt at that moment? His wife was telling him to send away his son Ishmael and his mother. The Bible records the pain he felt in those moments: "The matter distressed Abraham greatly because it concerned his son" (Genesis 21:11).

It is amazing how much pain comes from our choices in life. The incredible thing about our God is His grace and provision when we ask for forgiveness. We must live with the choices we have made in life but our choices will never be out of the reach of the forgiveness of our God. There will always be consequences to our sin but there is always forgiveness when we ask God.

> *We must live with the choices we have made in life but our choices will never be out of the reach of the forgiveness of our God.*

We can all relate to that. Many times we just think, "If I could only turn back the hands of time, I would live life differently." I know so many people who are in their forties who are living with the choices they made as teens. No matter how much we desire to turn back the sands of time, we can never do it, but we can walk forward in our relationship with Christ. We can just be assured in the faithfulness of God.

God provided for Abraham in his time of distress just as he will for each of us. "But God said to him, Do not be so distressed about the boy and your maidservant. Listen to whatever Sarah tells you, because it is through Isaac that your offspring will be reckoned. I will make the son of the maidservant into a nation also, because he is your offspring" (Genesis 21:12-13). It is good to know that God can work even through our poor choices in life. The choices we make do not limit God; they just limit the doors of opportunity in our lives.

"Early the next morning Abraham took some food and a skin of water and gave them to Hagar. He set them on her shoulders and then sent her off with the boy. She went on her way and wandered in the desert of Beersheba" (Genesis 21:14). Imagine the pain Abraham must have felt in his heart at that moment. He must have thought about how his choices were affecting Hagar and his son Ishmael. Surely in that moment, he wished he could turn back the hands of time. He must have also been comforted in knowing that God was providing for Hagar and Ishmael. God had told him that his son Ishmael would be made into a nation too.

Abraham had to live with his choices in life, but so did Hagar as well. "When the water in the skin was gone, she put the boy under one of the bushes. Then she went off and sat down nearby, about a bowshot away, for she thought, 'I cannot watch the boy die.' And as she sat there nearby, she began to sob" (Genesis 21:15-16). In that moment she too must have thought, "If I could only turn back the hands of time." God provided grace for her choices in her time of need. "God heard the boy crying, and the angel of God called to Hagar from heaven and said to her, 'What is the matter, Hagar? Do not be afraid; God has heard the boy crying as he lies there. Lift the boy up and take him by the hand, for I will make him into a great nation.' Then God opened her eyes and she saw a well of water. So she went and filled the skin with water and gave the boy a drink. God was with the boy as he grew up" (Genesis 21:17-20a).

Notice who was not experiencing the pain of their

choices in the passages above. Sarah! It was Sarah who told Abraham to go and sleep with her maid-servant Hagar, but it was Abraham and Hagar who had to live with the consequences of their choices. It is not the people who tell us to go through a supposed "door of opportunity" that have to live with the out-come of our choices. It is only us! When we listen to the world, and choose their way instead of God's way, it is we who live with the out come of our choices.

> *When we listen to the world, and choose their way instead of God's way, it is we who live with the out come of our choices.*

I am not saying that when we choose to go through doors that God has not opened for us, we should blame the world for our choices. Ultimately it is our choice to go the way of the world or God's way. In turn, we must personally take responsibility for our actions and live with the choices we make in life. We all make mistakes. Remember though, that when we mess up in life, God will forgive us if we will confess our sins to him.

*Trying to open doors on your own hinders God's grace.*

## CHAPTER TWELVE

# Let Your Journey Begin

$A$s we looked at this journey, we have seen the incredible faithfulness of God. As in the last chapter we have also seen the effects and pain of trying to open our own doors of opportunity. The temptation is there, but at all costs, we must always choose God's way over our own desires. No matter how good our intentions are, we must wait for God to open the doors of opportunity in our lives.

*The most important door of opportunity that any person can walk through is that of accepting Christ as their Lord and Savior!*

Although when we choose our own way, we must be reminded that God will forgive us when we ask and that He can still work through our choices in life.

The purpose of this book has been to help encourage each of us to live life in such a way that God can open doors of opportunity through normal, ordinary events in our lives. Through these pages you have been encouraged to grow deeper in your personal relationship with Christ. The most important door of opportunity that any person can walk through is that of accepting Christ as their Lord and Savior!

Be assured that, on this journey of life God provides for us his best in our life. Dr. Tony Evans, a pastor in the Dallas, Texas area, tells of a champion chess player. He was touring in Europe which included visiting many of the famous art collections. One day as he was going through a museum which contained priceless art work, his atten-

*When it seems like there are no more moves left, remember that God has always the last move.*

tion was captured by one painting. It depicted a chess game, and the title of the painting was Checkmate. There was depicted one man who had the look of defeat on his face while the winner was depicted as the devil. The devil was smiling and happy because the look on the man's face told the story. He had no move.

For an extended period of time this chess champion stood there looking at the painting. He asked if someone could get him a table and a chess set. When they provided it he laid the pieces on the board as depicted in the painting. For hours he studied the chess board. He finally said in an excited voice, "Sir, you still have one last move!" That move would win the game.

When it seems like there are no more moves left, remember that God has always the last move. When the doors in your life seem painted shut and the spirits of darkness are surrounding you, remember that God is in control. He does not desire for us to live a defeated life. When it seems like you have reached your end, remember, He makes the last move.

As you begin, or continue, your journey of God opening doors of opportunity in life, I challenge you to meditate on the following verses. If you put them into your memory it will help in those times when you are about to choose the way of the world over the ways of God. "Being confident of this, that he who began a good work in you will carry it on to completion until the day of Christ" (Philippians 1:6). "And we know that in all things God works for the good of those who love him, who have been called according to his purpose" (Romans 8:28).

> *If you will be faithful in writing down the journey of your spiritual life, you will be amazed, as you look back through it and see how many God Moments In Time you have truly encountered.*

As you continue on this journey, keep a journal of your spiritual life. I can hear what the guys are saying; "I am not keeping a diary." It is not a diary! It is a journal. If you will be faithful in writing down the journey of your spiritual life, you will be amazed, as you look back through it and see how many God Moments In Time you have truly encountered.

Know this: I will be praying for each person who reads the pages of this book that you will live your life so that God will open doors of opportunity that will change the direction of your life and impact eternity forever. May you experience many God Moments In Time in your life!

If you would like to share with me your God Moments in Time please feel free to contact me in any of the following ways.

**ProActive Faith Ministries™, Inc.**
PO Box 2394
Oklahoma City, OK 73101
www.proactivefaith.org
MyGodMomentStory@proactivefaith.org

Also you may click the link on our website
"God Moments In Time™ -- My Story"

*Faith without works
is dead!
May God grant you
success for your
journey!*

# *Notes*

## Chapter One

[1] Dwight "Ike" Reighard, OverComing Your Giants, excerpt from sermon, October , 1995, cassette.

[2] Russ Busby, Billy Graham God's Ambassador (Alexandria: Time-Life Books, 1999), 63.

## Chapter Four

[1] Thomas Brewer, CRUNCH Time Leader's Guide (Oklahoma City: ProActive Faith Publishing, 2002), 10.

[2] John MacArthur, The MacArthur Study Bible (Nashville: Thomas Nelson, 1997), 47.

## Chapter Nine

[1] www.gospelcom.net/chi/DAILYF/2003/04/daily-04-21-2003.shtml

[2] www.wheaton.edu/bgc/archives/faq/13.htm

# Discussion Questions

**Chapter One**

What are the areas of your life that are causing the doors of opportunity not to open?

What doors of opportunity has God opened in your life?

What events in your life have been "God Moments?"

Who have you seen in your life be faithful to God in the small things?

What were the spiritual qualities of these people who impacted your life?

**Chapter Two**

What was the promise made to Abraham?

Why did the promise of the son seem impossible?

What are some promises in your life that seem impossible?

What are areas in your life where it seems that God is testing your faithfulness?

Like the ram for Abraham, what provision has God made in your life

## Chapter Three

Why did Abraham choose his servant to find Isaac a bride?

Why did the servant have to make a vow concerning Abraham's wishes?

What are some situations in which you have asked God for clarification?

What are some reasons for asking God questions?

What is your level of commitment when God opens doors of opportunity?

## Chapter Four

What did the servant take on his journey?

What were some of the challenges of his journey?

What are you doing to prepare your life for the doors of opportunity?

As you prepare for your journeys in life what are some areas you personally need to work on?

In what ways have you seen God grant you success?

## Chapter Five

What was the daily task which Rebekah was doing when God opened her door of opportunity?

What were the acts of kindness Rebekah showed to the servant?

What are some acts of kindness people have shown to you?

What acts of kindness have you shown to people who want your time and effort?

What are some times where God has opened doors of opportunity in your life through the kindness of others?

**Chapter Six**

What did the servant do in response to God's faithfulness?

What are some times which you gave praise to things other than God?

What are some times in your life when God has opened doors of opportunity for which you gave him praise?

What can you do to make God's desire for your life known to the people around you?

In what ways can you show people around you kindness?

## Chapter Seven

What was the family's response to the servant wanting to return home?

What was the servant's response to the family?

What was Rebekah's response to her family?

What are some of the challenges you have faced when God has opened doors of opportunity in your life?

What are some times when you have followed God when it was not what your family or friends desired and how did you know that it was God opening the door?

**Chapter Eight**

What was the reward of the servant's successful journey?

What are the rewards you have experienced after your successful journeys?

What are some times in which you were led to pray specifically for someone?

What are some distractions you have faced on your journeys in life?

What were your emotions/excitement when God rewarded your journey?

## Chapter Nine

What is the present day reward of the faithful servant?

Who are some people you have seen who have made an impact on eternity?

In what ways are you presently being faithful with your doors of opportunity?

What times have you trusted God even when you did not see the "big picture?"

Discuss the "character" or faithfulness of God in your life.

**Chapter Ten**

What are some areas in your life in which you
have had to allow God to open the door?



What can you do to prepare for your God
Moments?



When did you ask Jesus Christ to be your personal Lord and Savior?



Why is it important to be connected to a group of
fellow believers?



Why is spending time alone with God key as you
prepare for your God moments?

## Chapter Eleven

What did Abraham do with Hagar that resulted in him opening his own door?

What were the results of Abraham's actions?

Who suggested that Abraham sleep with Hagar? How did Sarah respond to the situation?

What times have you been guilty of opening your own doors of opportunity?

How has God demonstrated his grace in the times when you have opened your own doors?

## Chapter Twelve

What are you planning to do as you begin or continue your journey?

How do you plan to grow deeper in your relationship with God?

What verses do you plan to meditate on as God opens doors of opportunity in your life?

What do you hope to see God do in your life in the days, months, and years to come?

How can you help people on their journey of experiencing God Moments?